NOTES TO READING THIS HANDBOOK

There is NO such thing as a standard lease. A lease is an agreement made by two or more parties to regulate the terms of the operation of goods or property for a term of 1 year to 999 years and bearing in mind that the various parties may be substituted *ad infinitum*.

Ideally you should read the whole of the Handbook and then keep it as a reference work to check on various aspects of the Lease from time to time. Because I am very much used to reading and writing such difficult documents, I have developed the ability to read the Handbook in one go. As it is so important, I would suggest that you read ten pages at a time and then take a break as your concentration fades. Then return later for another ten pages. Possibly you may wish to flick read the whole before consigning it to the bookshelf.

You should adopt the same approach when looking at your Lease itself.

LEASES CAN SERIOUSLY DAMAGE YOUR WEALTH

LEASES OF FLATS
In England and Wales

Laurie Norman
Lease Consultant

Copyright © 2021 Laurie Norman

The moral right of the author has been asserted.

Apart from any fair dealing for the purposes of research or private study, or criticism or review, as permitted under the Copyright, Designs and Patents Act 1988, this publication may only be reproduced, stored or transmitted, in any form or by any means, with the prior permission in writing of the publishers, or in the case of reprographic reproduction in accordance with the terms of licences issued by the Copyright Licensing Agency. Enquiries concerning reproduction outside those terms should be sent to the publishers.

Whilst every effort has been made to ensure that the details in this Handbook are correct, readers must be aware that the law changes and that the accuracy of the material cannot be guaranteed and the author and the publisher accept no responsibility for any losses or damage sustained.

This Handbook has been written on the basis of the law within England and Wales as at December 2020.

Matador
9 Priory Business Park,
Wistow Road, Kibworth Beauchamp,
Leicestershire. LE8 0RX
Tel: 0116 279 2299
Email: books@troubador.co.uk
Web: www.troubador.co.uk/matador
Twitter: @matadorbooks

ISBN 978 1800463 806

British Library Cataloguing in Publication Data.
A catalogue record for this book is available from the British Library.

Printed and bound by CPI Group (UK) Ltd, Croydon, CR0 4YY
Typeset in 11pt Ten Old Style by Troubador Publishing Ltd, Leicester, UK

Matador is an imprint of Troubador Publishing Ltd

CONTENTS

Introduction		ix
Chapter 1:	What have you bought?	1
	General	1
	Recommended Action	3
Chapter 2:	The Lease	5
	Lease Definitions	5
	Main Lease Provisions	7
Chapter 3:	The Parties	9
	General	9
Chapter 4:	The Extent of the Demised Premises	11
	General	11
	Recommended Action	13
Chapter 5:	The Extent of the Building/Estate	14
	General	14
	Recommended Action	14
Chapter 6:	The Term	16
	General	16

	Extending the Lease Term	16
	Potential Reforms	18
	Recommended Action	18
Chapter 7:	The Ground Rent payable	20
	General	20
	Rent Review Provisions	20
	Potential Reforms re level of Ground Rent	21
	Problem re Ground 8 of Second Schedule to Housing Act 1988	22
	Potential Reforms to resolve that problem	23
	Recommended Action	23
Chapter 8:	The Service Charge	24
	General	24
	Enhanced Rights of the Leaseholder	26
	Section 20 Procedure	26
	Potential Reforms of Section 20 Procedure	27
	Service Charge Financial Year	29
	Reserve or Sinking Funds	30
	Potential Reforms re Reserve or Sinking Funds	30
	Recommended Action	30
Chapter 9:	Insurance Rent	32
	General	32
	Potential Reforms	33
	Recommended Action	33
Chapter 10:	Leaseholder's Covenants	34
	Repair and Redecoration	34
	Use	35
	Alterations	35
	Disposals	36
	Administration Charges	38

	Leasehold Property Enquiry Form	39
	Potential Reforms re sale of Leaseholds	39
	Exit or Event Fees	40
	Potential Reforms re Exit or Event Fees	40
	Payment of Landlord's costs	41
	Interest	41
	To Permit Entry	41
	Dos and Don'ts	42
	Recommended Action	42
Chapter 11:	Breach of Covenant by a Leaseholder	43
	Actions available to the Landlord	43
	Forfeiture	44
	Potential Reforms	45
Chapter 12:	Landlord's Covenants	46
	General	46
Chapter 13:	Management Company Covenants	48
	General	48
Chapter 14:	Notices	50
	General	50
Chapter 15:	Dispute Resolution	51
	First Tier Tribunal	51
	Potential Reforms	52
Chapter 16:	Matters beyond the Lease	53
	Recognised Tenants Associations	53
	Statutory Provisions which benefit Leaseholders	54
	Landlord and Tenant Act 1985	54
	Landlord and Tenant Act 1987 (as amended by the Housing Act 1996)	55

	The Leasehold Reform, Housing and Urban Development Act 1993	56
	The Commonhold and Leasehold Reform Act 2002	56
	Right to Manage Companies ("RTM")	57
	Potential Reforms re RTM	58
	Recommended Action	58
Chapter 17:	Managing Agents	59
	General	59
	Potential Reforms	61
	Recommended Action	61
Chapter 18:	Cladding on Buildings – post Grenfell	62
	General	62
	Potential Reforms	65
	Recommended Action	66
Chapter 19:	Making Landlord and Tenant Law Easier	68
	Potential Reforms	69

INTRODUCTION

I was a practising lawyer for nearly 40 years specialising almost exclusively in Leases (both residential and commercial) – in that time I have acted for Leaseholders, Landlords and Management Companies; drafted Leases and associated documentation; approved and amended them and dealt with the sale and purchases of Leasehold property. I have also made successful applications to the Leasehold Valuation Tribunal on behalf of Leaseholders in relation to unreasonable Service Charges.

In addition, I have worked for and provided advice to Property Managers and Managing Agents in relation to the management of leasehold properties and have seen wide-ranging differences in their attempts to interpret Lease provisions, particularly in relation to Service Charges.

All that experience has given me a unique insight into Leasehold Law (from both sides of the fence) including how it works in practice and the day-to-day interpretation and operation of it.

Whilst I cannot explain why, I love working with Leases, have a real passion for them, and have been very lucky to have been able to spend my career working with something I really enjoy. It seems only right for me to now pass on to Leaseholders the benefit of my knowledge and experience.

There is a widespread feeling that, in many cases, Leaseholders of Flats are short-changed, unfairly treated and need better protection. The Government have now taken the initiative and are setting about reforming Landlord and Tenant Law and they have started 2021 with a commitment to introduce legislation to bring Ground Rents in new Leases down to zero and then follow that up with much wider legislation (to include the right for Leaseholders to extend their Leases up to 990 years). Major developers have also been moving to zero ground rents on new Leasehold developments and Lenders are refusing to lend money on Leasehold Properties which have unfair rent review clauses.

There is now a clear wind of change blowing even though it will still be some time before all of such changes are made.

The first line of defence for any Leaseholder is to know exactly what your own Lease says and what rights you currently have available to address matters which concern you. Don't assume that your Landlord or Management Company will automatically follow what the Lease says. Doing nothing is the enemy of the Leaseholder.

This Handbook, in plain English, guides the Leaseholder through the terms of a Lease and explains what rights they already have to protect them and how to use them to their advantage, as well as making them aware of proposed changes. Obtaining formal legal advice is extremely expensive, but this Handbook gives Leaseholders the information that they need at a fraction of the cost

Further information and assistance is available on my web site:

www.leaseconsult.co.uk

Chapter 1

What Have You Bought?

Great – you have bought your Flat and have picked up the keys – you remember your lawyer telling you that you were buying a Leasehold property and you were sent a bundle of documents, which you had a brief look at, but hardly understood a word of them!

You are, in fact, the proud owner of a Lease of the Flat – a Lease is a binding document (like a contract) made between:

1. The Landlord (usually the Freeholder of the Building of which the Flat forms a part)
2. The original Leaseholder (i.e. the person who first bought the Flat)
3. The Management Company (although some Leases do not have a Management Company as a party to them and it is the Landlord who is responsible for keeping the building in repair and providing the services)

All of the parties to the Lease enter into legally binding obligations with each other (known as "covenants") and those obligations are set out in the Lease. If the Leasehold interest in the Flat is sold, the buyer (i.e. the new owner of the Flat) becomes responsible for the performance of the Leaseholder's obligations.

In your case, you will have either bought a new Flat (and are therefore the original Leaseholder) or you have bought an existing Flat and, as the buyer, have taken over the original Leaseholder's obligations contained in the Lease.

Leases are by their very nature quite complicated documents (I have seen some less than 20 pages long and others at well over 100 pages) and, in my experience, they are not explained very well to the buyer when the property the subject of the Lease is purchased – many lawyers do not like working with Leases due to their length and complexity! The form of Leases vary considerably with each Developer/Landlord using their own 'pet' form at the time the Lease was granted, so this Handbook can only refer to Leases in general terms.

For the purposes of this Handbook, when I refer to a Lease it is to what is known as a 'Long Lease' (i.e. a Lease which had an original Lease Term of over 21 years when it was first granted).

At various points in this Handbook I make refence to the following:

- 'the First Tier Tribunal' – that is the First-Tier Tribunal (Property Chamber) in England or the Leasehold Valuation Tribunal in Wales, which are Tribunals established to determine disputes relating to property and which are intended to operate on a more 'informal' basis than the Courts
- 'the Pledge' – that is a pledge published in March 2019 by the Government and made by at least 62 leading property developers and freeholders to stop Leaseholders being trapped in unfair and costly deals. It mainly deals with rent review provisions in new Leases
- 'the Code' – that is the Service Charge Residential Management Code (3rd Edition) produced by the Royal Institution of Chartered

Surveyors (and approved by the Government) and generally aimed at managing agents, with a view to improving general standards and promote best practice, uniformity, reasonableness and transparency in the management and administration of long leasehold residential property

- 'ARMA' – the Association of Residential Managing Agents – these are the leading professional body for residential managing agents in England and Wales: *www.arma.org.uk*
- 'ARHM' – the Association of Retirement Housing Managers – these are the largest trade association body for the retirement sector: *www.arhm.org*
- 'CERTASS Scheme' – the Certass Competent Person Scheme operated by CERTASS Limited of PO Box 26332 Ayr KA7 9BJ: *www.certass.co.uk*
- 'FENSA Scheme' – the Fenestration Self-Assessment Scheme operated by FENSA Limited of 40 Rushworth Street London SE1 0RB: *www.fensa.org.uk*
- 'NHBC' – NHBC of NHBC House Davy Avenue Knowlhill Milton Keynes MK5 8FP are the UK's leading independent provider of warranty and insurance for new homes: *www.nhbc.co.uk*

RECOMMENDED ACTION

- Get to know your Lease
- Before you consider your own Lease in detail, it is important to establish whether the Lease has been varied in any way
- Do you know if any determinations have been made in relation to the Leases of other Flats within the same Building as your Flat by the Leasehold Valuation Tribunal or the First Tier Tribunal or if any such applications are pending?

- Check and keep copies of the Service Charge and other documentation you receive from the Landlord, the Management Company or their managing agents – they may come in useful later
- Discuss issues which concern you with other Leaseholders (a collective approach often works better) – attend meetings set up by Leaseholders within your Building to discuss issues arising – seek appropriate advice
- If you are a member of, or a Shareholder in, the Management Company, attend the Annual General Meeting of such Company and voice any concerns you may have

Chapter 2

The Lease

Most Leases contain a clause or clauses (usually near the beginning) which sets out the definitions of words or phrases used in the Lease itself and some of these clauses can be quite extensive. I will not go into detail with all of such definitions but the following words and phrases are particularly relevant:

- "Building" – the building of which the Demised Premises (i.e. the Flat) forms a part
- "Certificate" – the certificate to be issued to the Leaseholder by or on behalf of the Landlord or Management Company following the end of the Service Charge Financial Year and which usually gives a summary of the Service Charge expenditure incurred, the Service Charge payable by the Leaseholder and any balancing payment due after taking into account any advance payments made
- "Common Parts" – those parts of the Building and the Estate which are not included within any of the Leases granted (sometimes these may also be referred to as 'Retained Parts')

- "Covenants" – the obligations entered into by the respective parties as set out in the Lease (i.e. agreements to do or not to do certain things)
- "the Estate" – the Estate on which the Building and the Common Parts are situated
- "Demised Premises" – the property actually demised to the Leaseholder under the Lease (sometimes this might be called 'Premises' or 'Property')
- "Financial Year" – the period of one year over which the service charge expenditure is incurred (this will not necessarily be from 1st January to 31st December)
- "Insured Risks" – the risks against which the Building and Estate are insured against
- "Landlord" – usually the Freeholder of the Estate (sometimes they might be called 'Lessor')
- "Main Structures" – if there is such a definition then these are usually the structural parts of the Building which are not included in any demise to a Leaseholder
- "Management Company" – any Management Company which has been included as a party to the Lease to carry out the management functions – usually (but not always) this is set up by the Landlord at the time of the original development with a view to the Leaseholders then becoming members or shareholders of the Management Company and taking over the running of the Management Company
- "Service Charge" (sometimes called a 'Maintenance Charge') – this relates to the expenditure incurred by the Landlord or the Management Company in the management of the Building/Estate, their maintenance repair and redecoration and the provision of services to them – each Leaseholder will be responsible for paying a contribution towards the Service Charge
- "Service Charge Proportion" – the proportion of Service Charge

expenditure which is attributable to the Demised Premises and payable by the Leaseholder (sometimes an express % is specified in the Lease but very often it says something like 'the fair and proper proportion attributable to the Demised Premises', leaving it up to the Landlord or Management Company to calculate such proportion)

- "Tenant" – the person or persons to whom the Lease is granted (sometimes they might be called 'Lessee') – in this Handbook I refer to them as the Leaseholder
- "Term" – this is the term of years the Demised Premises have been demised to the Leaseholder and it is stated to commence on an express date (such as 99 years from 1st January 2020) and that date is known as the Commencement Date – that express date will be the reference point used in determining matters under the Lease such as when redecorating obligations or rent reviews fall due. The shorter the Term left on the Lease, the harder it will be to obtain mortgage finance (and that will affect the ability to sell), but the Leaseholder does have a statutory right to extend the Lease Term – see Chapter 6 for more information in relation to extending a Lease Term

Whilst the layout will be different for each development, the main provisions of a Lease, will be:

1. Description of the property actually demised to the Leaseholder
2. Payment of the Ground Rent (and any review of such Ground Rent), the Service Charge and, in some cases (where separate from the Service Charge), the Buildings Insurance premium
3. The rights granted for the benefit of the Leaseholder over other parts of the Building and the Common Parts of the Estate
4. The rights reserved to the Landlord, the Management Company and other Leaseholders over the property demised to the Leaseholder

5. The covenants entered into by the Leaseholder
6. The covenants entered into by the Landlord and (if there is one) the Management Company
7. Provisions dealing in detail with the Service Charge and the expenditure to be recoverable via the Service Charge
8. Provisions dealing with the insurance put in place by the Landlord or the Management Company in relation to the Building and the Estate and the means to recover the premium paid (either on its own or via the Service Charge)
9. Regulations to be observed by the Leaseholder (general do's and don'ts)
10. General provisions which would deal with such things as the Landlord's ability to forfeit the Lease for non-payment of rent or breach of covenant; how notices have to be served; dispute resolution and the like

We will now look at specific parts of a Lease.

Chapter 3

The Parties

This will be the Landlord and Tenant and there could also be a Management Company (in which case the Management Company will be responsible for the provision of most of the services to the Building and the Estate, such as maintenance, redecoration etc.). The Management Company's obligations could extend to effecting buildings insurance but in some cases the Landlord retains the right to deal with this and recover the cost separately from the Leaseholder.

Unless the Lease is completely new, it is possible that the identity of:

- the Landlord has changed (i.e. the original Landlord has subsequently sold off its interest in the Building/Estate)
- the Leaseholder has changed (i.e. the original owner of the Flat has sold it to a subsequent buyer)

It is also possible that (if there was one) the original Management Company is no longer involved in the management of the Building/Estate and that its functions have been taken over by a Right to Manage

Company ('RTM") appointed by the Leaseholders – see Chapter 16 for more information in relation to RTM Companies.

Chapter 4

The Extent of the Demised Premises

The extent of the Demised Premises (i.e. the Flat, which is usually shown edged red on the Lease plan and in many cases accompanied by a wider written description) is very important (but not every Lease sets this out in detail), as this will determine the extent of the Leaseholder's and the Landlord's or Management Company's respective repairing/redecorating obligations and also dictates the extent to which the Leaseholder can carry out alterations to the Flat. For example:

1.1 Does it include the windows and front door (very often it does)?

- What are the windows made of? – if they are UPVC and are included within the demise the Leaseholder will be responsible for their repair and replacement, with no decoration required – if they are wooden and included within the demise it could well be that whilst the Leaseholder is responsible for their repair

and replacement, the Landlord or Management Company is responsible for external decoration
- Is the Leaseholder permitted to replace such windows or front door? Is the prior consent of the Landlord or Management Company needed before the windows or front door can be changed and what type of windows or door will be acceptable?
- If the Leaseholder is responsible for the replacement of the front door to the Flat, they need to be aware that any new front door must comply with current Fire Regulations
- who is responsible for window cleaning (very often the Leaseholder cleans the inside and the Landlord or Management Company cleans the outside, with the cost of the latter being recoverable via the Service Charge)?

1.2 Is it a top floor flat – if so, is the loft space included/can it be used by the Leaseholder?

1.3 Is there a balcony/patio area – if so, what parts must the Leaseholder maintain and decorate?

1.4 Is a garage/parking space included? – if not, does the Leaseholder have the right to use a garage/parking space? Who is responsible for repair?

1.5 Is the Main Structure excluded? – this is very often the case and only the internal plaster on the external wall is included in the demise of the Flat – in such circumstances, the Leaseholder would not be able to instal, for instance, an extraction vent for better ventilation as that would need to pass through the external wall. The Landlord or the Management Company would have absolute control as to whether they would be prepared to allow the Leaseholder to do this

1.6 Is the Leaseholder prevented from laying wood or laminate flooring in the main areas of the Flat (which would create sound which could cause nuisance to the owner of the Flat underneath)?

> **RECOMMENDED ACTION**
>
> - Make sure that you know what is (and is not) included in the demise of the Flat
> - Repair and decorate those parts as appropriate
> - If you want to carry out alterations make sure you get the Landlord's or the Management Company's consent where needed (if you ever come to sell your Flat the buyer will want to see any such consents and it can be expensive to obtain retrospective consent)

Chapter 5

The Extent of the Building/Estate

This needs to be made clear in the Lease, as this will show how many other properties comprise the Building/Estate (very often the respective boundaries of the Building and the Estate are shown by coloured lines on the Lease plan).

It will also determine who else should be contributing towards the Service Charge (there may be Flats, Houses and/or commercial premises on the Estate) – it could well be that there are different Service Charge Proportions applicable to different types of premises.

> **RECOMMENDED ACTION**
>
> - Establish who all the other contributors to the Service Charge are
> - Check the Service Charge demands and other documentation

The Extent of the Building/Estate

you received from the Landlord or the Management Company for evidence that they are all making such contributions

Chapter 6

The Term (i.e. the number of years you will own the Flat)

How long is the Lease Term and when did it commence?

Lease Terms for Leases of residential properties are very often 99, 125, 150, 250 or 999 years.

As mentioned before, the Commencement Date will be the reference point used in determining matters under the Lease such as when redecorating obligations or rent reviews under the Lease fall due.

The shorter the term left on the Lease, the harder it will be to obtain mortgage finance (and that will affect to ability to sell). Many lenders providing mortgage finance on leasehold property require there to be a period of around 25 or 30 years of the Lease term remaining after the mortgage period has expired – that would mean if a buyer took out, for instance, a 30 year mortgage then at the time of the purchase the Lease would need to have a minimum unexpired term of around 60 years (although many lenders require it to be longer than this).

There are two ways in which a Lease Term can be extended:

The Term (i.e. the number of years you will own the Flat)

- voluntary – i.e. the Leaseholder reaches agreement with the Landlord to extend the Lease – it should be noted that the Landlord is under no obligation to grant any such extension and can dictate what terms (if any) it would be prepared to do so (such as the premium (i.e. the purchase price) to be payable to the Landlord by the Leaseholder, the length of the extended Term, any new Ground Rent to be paid and payment of the Landlord's costs)
- by using the defined statutory procedure (which, currently, the Leaseholder can only do once they have held the Lease for two years or more) – this would result in an extension Lease being granted on the following basis:

   a. for the present unexpired Lease Term plus an additional 90 years
   b. at a peppercorn rent (i.e. in effect no Ground Rent will then be payable).
   c. be on the same terms as the existing Lease, subject to minor modifications and certain statutory exclusions and additions.
   d. a premium would be payable by the Leaseholder to the Landlord (based upon a statutory valuation formula)
   e. the Leaseholder would have to pay the Landlord's reasonable professional costs (usually solicitors and surveyors) in relation to the Lease Term extension.

Once a Lease Term falls below 80 years then the amount to be paid to extend the Term increases dramatically. Whilst Landlords are reluctant to enter a voluntary agreement to extend the Term of such Leases (because they will get much more when the term falls below 80 years), there is no reason why the statutory procedure cannot be exercised to extend the Term of a Lease having an unexpired Term of more than 80 years.

More information in relation to Lease extensions can be found on my web site: www.leaseconsult.co.uk

Potential Reforms

It has been proposed by the Law Commission that :

- the requirement that the Leaseholder has owned the Flat for two years be removed (so the Leaseholder would be able to make a claim for a Lease Term extension at any time)
- there should be introduced a more simplified basis to assess the premium to be paid by the Leaseholder to the Landlord for a Lease Term extension, to arrive at a premium set at a level which properly balances the respective interests of the Landlord and the Leaseholder and which overcomes (or substantially reduces) the need for mediation tribunals

In early January 2021, the Government announced that it intends to:

- give Leaseholders the right to extend their Leases up to a Term of 990 years and with no Ground Rent being payable
- introduce a simplified calculation method for calculating the premium (purchase price) to be paid by a Leaseholder to their Landlord for a Lease Extension, so as to ensure that this is fairer, cheaper and more transparent
- introduce an online calculator to make it simpler for Leaseholders to find out how much it will cost them to extend their Lease (or buy their Freehold)
- introduce further reforming legislation in due course

RECOMMENDED ACTION

- Even if you are not proposing to sell your Flat, it is worth checking the length of the Term of your Lease and see

The Term (i.e. the number of years you will own the Flat)

how many years are remaining. Whilst, at present, it is not very usual for Leaseholders with a Lease Term remaining which exceeds 80 years to seek to extend their Lease, there is no reason why it cannot be extended and the premium payable will be less than for an extension of a Lease Term below 80 years – some Landlords may not be willing to enter into voluntary negotiations for such an extension, but the statutory procedure could still be used (which, if based upon a remaining term of 80 years, would result on the extended Lease Term being for 170 years – the extended Lease Term will mean that the value of your Flat will rise

- If you are interested in the possibility of extending your Lease Term, then seek formal advice as to the likely premium payable and the costs involved before starting the process
- Make a check against the Landlord's Freehold Title to the Building to see whether they have already extended the Term of any Leases within the Building (which, if recently done, would give you an indication of the amount the Leaseholder of that Flat had to pay for such Lease Term extension)

Chapter 7

The Ground Rent Payable

What is the annual Ground Rent payable – it could be:

- a 'peppercorn' rent (i.e. in effect, no ground rent is payable at all)
- a fixed annual sum payable throughout the Term
- an annual sum which is subject to review at specified intervals throughout the Term – some rent reviews provide for fixed increases at each review (such as the Ground Rent doubling at each review) and others provide for any increase to be determined by rises in the Retail Prices Index (i.e. the index used to calculate cost of living and wage escalation), which would lead to significantly lower increases of Ground Rent

Rent review provisions in residential Leases have become a 'hot' topic, with many providing for the Ground Rent to double at regular intervals (leaving the Leaseholder being faced with the payment of onerous and unsustainable Ground Rents). Such rent review provisions are now meeting resistance in the market place and considered to be unfair, which has led to the following:

- Lenders not providing mortgage finance on Leases which contain rent review provisions which will lead to unreasonable increases at rent review (such as where the Ground Rent doubles) – the UK Lenders Finance Handbook, which sets out the requirements of Lenders providing mortgage finance, requires Ground Rents to be 'predictable, to be understood as to what the level is going to be, to be set out quite clearly, and to allow that to increase periodically by a reasonable amount'
- Major property developers giving the Pledge
- The UK Government seeking to introduce appropriate legislation.

As a result, it is now becoming common for Leaseholders (when they are seeking to sell their property) being asked by the buyers to get the Landlord, where appropriate, to vary the rent review provisions contained in the Lease in order to enable mortgage funding to be obtained by the buyer – ultimately legislation is likely to be enacted to deal with such rent reviews but, until then, a document known as a Deed of Variation would be needed (which if the Landlord is prepared to enter one (not all will) then they will require that their costs are paid).

In December 2020 it was announced that five of the UK's biggest housebuilders had scrapped Ground Rents for Leases on new Flats and it is most likely that others will follow suit, in view of the potential reforms outlined below.

Potential Reforms

In the cases of new Leases being granted (but with some exceptions), the Government, in early 2021 announced its intention to bring forward in the then upcoming session of Parliament legislation to set future Ground Rents to zero (i.e. no Ground Rent will be payable). This will also apply to retirement Leasehold properties

The above proposed reforms will, however, only benefit those Leaseholders who are taking a new Lease. The position is more difficult in the case of existing Leases as the Government have not expressed any present plans to introduce legislation in relation to existing Leases, other than relying upon the Pledge and committing to monitor the actions of the industry, then taking further action as necessary – that is not much use to the leaseholders of existing Leasehold Flats within England and Wales (of which there are estimated to be in the region of 3 million), as the vast majority of them will not have Freeholders/Landlords who have given the Pledge

Market forces are, however, starting to influence the position in relation to existing Leases, with (as mentioned above) Lenders not being prepared to provide mortgage finance on Leases which have unreasonable Ground Rent review clauses and requiring such Leases to be varied. Those market forces are likely to gather even more momentum with the proposed new legislation

A technical issue has also recently arisen in relation to Ground Rents and Ground 8 of Schedule 2 of the Housing Act 1988, which allows the Landlord to make an application to the Court for possession of the Flat where three months' Ground Rent is at least 3 months in arrear – once such an application has been made the Court cannot refuse to grant an order for possession, as Ground 8 is mandatory – this has caused alarm to mortgage lenders as it introduces the prospect of them losing their security and, as a result, many are not willing to provide mortgage finance for the purchase of Flats which are held under a Lease which could be affected.

Once again, it is now becoming common for Leaseholders (when they are seeking to sell their property) being asked by the buyers to get the Landlord, where appropriate, to vary the Lease in order to overcome this issue – ultimately legislation is likely to be enacted to resolve this problem but, until then a Deed of Variation will be required (which most Landlords are happy to enter into providing that their costs are paid).

Potential Reforms

The Government has recognised the Ground 8 problem and has said that it is proposing to address the issue by introducing legislation to exempt leaseholders from Ground 8 possession claims, but this remains to be done

RECOMMENDED ACTION

- Check what Ground Rent is payable under your Lease
- Check at what intervals such Ground Rent is to be reviewed and the basis upon which such review is to take place
- If your Lease is likely to be affected by the above, it might be worth approaching the Landlord to see if they are prepared to vary your Lease (particularly if you are thinking of selling) – if you are a member of a Management Company which already owns the Freehold to your Building (and the Leases have not already been extended), then a collective approach (which would save costs) could be adopted with a view to all of the Leases within the Building being suitably varied (possibly with an extension of the Lease Term as well)
- Make a check against the Landlord's Freehold Title to the Building to see whether they have already entered into any such variations of the Leases of other Flats within your building (in which case they may well have set a precedent)

Chapter 8

The Service Charge

The Service Charge is the means by which the Landlord or Management Company obtain the funds to maintain the Building and the Estate and they are dependent upon receipt of the Service Charge monies from the Leaseholders to enable them to comply with their obligations contained in the Lease and to provide the services.

Each Leaseholder (and possibly other occupiers on the Estate such as the owners of Freehold Houses) will be required to contribute towards the Service Charge.

What is the Service Charge Proportion payable by the Leaseholder? – does it follow what is set out in the Lease (it should be noted that this proportion will dictate what the Leaseholder is required to contribute and not what parts of the Building/Estate the Leaseholder may or may not use) – if a fixed % is set out in the Lease, does the Service Charge demand correspond with such % – if not, why not?

Many Leases (but not all) give the Landlord or the Management Company the ability to vary the Service Charge Proportion payable by the Leaseholder in certain circumstances and provided that it is done on a fair and reasonable basis.

If the Service Charge Proportion has changed, the Landlord or the Management Company must be able to provide details of the reasons for such a change and the basis upon which such change was made.

It is clearly important that the Landlord or Management Company is able to recover 100% of the Service Charge expenditure as permitted by the Lease. That is why it is necessary to have adequate information as to how many properties comprise the Building and the Estate and the obligations imposed upon them to contribute towards the Service Charge – it may well be that different properties contribute different proportions towards the Service Charge – for example, Leasehold Flats may well pay a higher proportion as they are part of the Building (which will require more maintenance) whereas Freehold Houses will pay a lesser proportion as they will only contribute towards the Common Parts of the Estate (as they maintain their own Houses).

When Leases are originally granted the Landlord or the Management Company can use different methods of assessing the Service Charge contributions such as:

- All Leaseholders paying the same contribution
- The level of each Leaseholder's % contribution being determined by the number of bedrooms the relevant property has
- The level of each Leaseholder's % contribution being determined by the floor area the relevant property has
- What facilities are used by the relevant Leaseholder/Freeholder

The Lease will set out what obligations the Landlord, the Management Company and the Leaseholder have in relation to the Service Charge. It will also set out what expenditure is recoverable via the Service Charge (which could include legal and other costs incurred by the Landlord or Management Company – if there is no express provision for it then the Landlord or Management Company may not be able to recover that expense).

In addition, there have been numerous Acts of Parliament which have enhanced the rights of Leaseholders covering matters such as the following:

- That a Service Charge is only recoverable so far as the costs have been reasonably incurred and the works the subject of the charge are of a reasonable standard – the Leaseholder is able to challenge the reasonableness of Service Charges at the First Tier Tribunal

    It should, however, be noted that a Leaseholder cannot make such a challenge against Service Charges which:

    1. the Leaseholder has already agreed or admitted responsibility for paying
    2. have been (or will be) referred to arbitration following a dispute or
    3. have already been decided by a Court or Tribunal

- Certain ("Section 20") procedures (which can take several months to complete) under which the Landlord or the Management Company have to consult with Leaseholders in relation to:

    1. works proposed to be carried out to the Building/Estate where the cost of such works (including VAT) will exceed £250 for any one Leaseholder (i.e. under the Service Charge the Leaseholder will have to pay more than £250 in relation to such works) or
    2. long term agreements (i.e. agreements for a period of more than 12 months) proposed to be entered into by the Landlord or the Management Company where the amount payable by any one contributing Leaseholder under such agreement in any one year exceeds £100 (including VAT) (i.e. under the

Service Charge the Leaseholder will have to pay more than £100 in relation to such agreement)
3. where any such long term agreement includes provision for the carrying out of works to the Building/Estate and such works will result in the cost of such works (including VAT) exceeding £250 for any one leaseholder, then a separate consultation procedure must be carried out with the Leaseholders

If any of these consultation procedures are not followed by the Landlord or the Management Company then the expenditure incurred may not be recoverable from the Leaseholders, although it is possible for the Landlord or the Management Company in appropriate circumstances (such as where emergency repairs may be needed) to apply to the First Tier Tribunal for a determination to dispense with the consultation requirements, where it would be reasonable to do so.

Potential Reforms to Section 20 procedures

The Government is proposing to review the consultation process outlined above with a view to, ideally, major works and associated costs being planned and notified to Leaseholders well in advance, thereby reducing the need for multiple one-off consultations

- Requirements as to the form Service Charge demands must take – they must contain the Landlord's name and address (an agent's name and address is not sufficient) and must also include a 'summary of Leaseholder's rights and obligations' (which would include reference to the Leaseholder's right to apply to the First Tier Tribunal to challenge the reasonableness of a Service Charge). If the Service Charge demands are not issued in the proper manner

then the Leaseholder has a legal right not to pay unless and until the Service Charge is demanded in the proper manner
- A limitation upon the period for the recovery of Service Charge costs – Service Charge costs that were incurred more than 18 months before they are demanded from the Leaseholder cannot be recovered (although they will still be recoverable if the Landlord or the Management Company has written to the Leaseholder within 18 months of incurring such costs informing them that they have incurred such costs, giving details of the amount of costs and stating that such costs will be demanded in due course)

Most residential Leases provide for a Leaseholder to (1) make payments in advance to the Landlord or the Management Company towards the Service Charge (usually either annually, half-yearly or quarterly), based upon an estimate of the likely Service Charge costs and (2) at the end of the relevant Financial Year once those costs have been determined and Service Charge accounts prepared (and in some cases audited), to make a 'balancing up' payment if the expenditure has exceeded the estimate or, if the Leaseholder has overpaid then for the Landlord or the Management Company to carry forward the amount overpaid for the benefit of the Leaseholder to the following Financial Year. It is now quite rare to find a Lease where the Service Charge is payable in arrears (i.e. the Landlord or the Management Company has to incur the expenditure before being able to recover it via the Service Charge).

The Lease will set out what documentation the Landlord or the Management Company has to provide the Leaseholder with at the end of the Service Charge Financial Year to support the Service Charge demand – very often that will be a Certificate accompanied by details of the annual expenditure, details of the Service Charge payable by the Leaseholder and a demand showing what (if any) balancing payment is due (having taken into account any advance payments of Service Charge made by the Leaseholder).

Whilst ultimately the provisions set out in the Lease dictate how the Service Charge is to be paid by the Leaseholder, many Management Companies (although they are under no obligation to do so) do allow Leaseholders to pay the Service Charge by regular monthly payments by standing order. They are not, however, obliged to do so (unless the Lease expressly provides for this) and the specific requirements set out in the Lease will always prevail.

The Service Charge Financial Year is usually set out in the Lease, although some Leases do give the Landlord or the Management Company the ability to change this – in some cases the Lease sets out what steps the Landlord or the Management Company must take before they can change the Service Charge Financial Year – the Landlord or the Management Company can only change the Service Charge Financial Year if the Lease allows for it.

The Lease may also set out a timescale within which year end accounts are to be produced to the Leaseholder, but many do not and there is no statutory requirement for annual statements (based upon the year end accounts) to be issued within any specific timescale.

The Code suggests that year end accounts should be prepared and provided within 6 months of the end of the relevant Financial Year, which ought to be a reasonable time period but very often that is not the case – delayed accounts have a 'knock on' effect to the collection of any Service Charge shortfalls or the carrying forward of overpayments for the benefit of Leaseholders and also complicate the sale of a Leasehold property where up to date Service Charge information is not available, leading to the need for monies being retained by the buyer to cover potential future Service Charge Liability once the Year End accounts have been finalised. It is not unheard of for year end accounts to be a couple of years late!

In its guidance to Managing Agents, ARMA also suggest that it is best practice in relation to year end accounts to issue all annual statements within six months of the end of the relevant Financial Year.

The Service Charge provisions in most Leases provide for the

Landlord or the Management Company to collect and set aside monies to build up a 'reserve fund' or 'sinking fund' for the purpose of accumulating a sum of money to cover the cost of irregular and expensive work, such as decorating the outside of the building, carrying out major structural repairs (such as roof replacement) or replacing the lift – whilst this increases the Service Charge payable by the Leaseholder, if you think about it, providing that sum is reasonable then it is in the interests of all Leaseholders to have such a reserve fund. Without such a fund then, should items of major expenditure be needed, the Leaseholders will have to make a major contribution towards such costs all in one go!

Potential Reforms re reserve funds/sinking funds

The Government are considering the suggestions that (1) reserve funds/sinking funds should be made mandatory in both new and existing Leases and (2) they consider by what means it can be ensured that such funds are effectively funded

Finally, if the Flat was formerly a Council owned property then it might be occupied under what is known as a 'right to buy' Lease, in which case there may then be additional provisions which apply such as a cap on the level of service charge that can be recovered from the Leaseholder.

RECOMMENDED ACTION

- Consider the Service Charge demands and associated documentation you receive very carefully
- Check that the demands comply with the requirements outlined above
- Check what Service Charge % you are being asked to pay – does it accord with that set out in your Lease?

- Check that there is a Reserve Fund
- Be realistic about the level of the Service Charge – it might be nice to pay very little, but if you pay little, you will get little done and will be faced with large bills as and when works are required (or, if no work is done, the condition of the Building will deteriorate, making it less attractive and ultimately reduce the value of your Flat) – it is always better for the Building to be managed on the basis of a program of planned maintenance in order to ensure the ongoing condition of the Building and also (as far as possible) to level out the Service Charge from year to year

Chapter 9

Insurance Rent

It is usual for the Landlord or the Management Company to arrange the buildings insurance in respect of the Building and Estate of which the Flat forms a part and very often the cost of effecting that insurance is recovered as part of the Service Charge.

However, in some Leases the Landlord retains the right to put such insurance in place and recover the cost from the Leaseholders separately to the Service Charge. The % contributions payable by the Leaseholder for this (or the basis upon which they are to be assessed) should be set out in the Lease – they are not always the same as the % contributions payable in respect of the Service Charge, depending upon the nature and extent of the Estate.

The Leaseholder has the right to ask the Landlord (once a year) for information in relation to the buildings insurance policy, by making a formal written request to the Landlord for a written summary, which should be sent to the Leaseholder free of charge – the summary should contain details of the sums for which the relevant property is insured, the name of the insurer and the risks covered by such policy. The Landlord has 21 days to respond.

The Leaseholder has the ability to challenge the cost of buildings insurance at the First Tier Tribunal, as with any other Service Charge cost, as outlined above. It should, however, be noted that the Landlord does not need to search the market for the cheapest quote – the insurance premium will generally be considered to be reasonable if the Landlord has 'tested the market' and sought an insurer in the open market on an arm's length basis (i.e. there is no special relationship between the Landlord and the insurance company).

It is for the Leaseholder to insure their own contents within the Flat.

Potential Reforms

The Government have been encouraged to look at regulating the area of commissions paid by insurance providers to Landlords to encourage the insurance business being placed with them (and which ultimately are passed on to the Leaseholders by way of higher premiums)

RECOMMENDED ACTION

- Consider the buildings insurance information you are provided with very carefully
- Check what % of the buildings insurance premium you are being asked to pay – does it accord with that set out in your Lease?
- Do some research and see if the buildings insurance premium reflects those available on the open market

Chapter 10

Leaseholder's Covenants

In the Lease the Leaseholder enters into various obligations (known as 'covenants') with the Landlord and/or the Management Company, such as to pay the Ground Rent, the Service Charge and the Insurance Rent.

I will not go into detail in relation to all of the Leaseholder covenants, as many are self-explanatory in any event, but such covenants will deal with many other things including matters such as:

1.1 Repair and Redecoration

What repairs and redecoration will be the responsibility of the Leaseholder – this will be governed by the extent of the Flat demised to the Leaseholder – assuming the main structure is excluded, which is often the case, the Leaseholder will usually be responsible for:

- the repair of internal non-structural parts
- the repair and replacement of the windows and front door
- redecoration of the interior of the Flat

On this basis, the Landlord or the Management Company would be responsible for the maintenance of the main structure and external redecoration, albeit with the Leaseholder contributing towards the cost via the Service Charge

1.2 Use – as a residential Flat

It is sometimes limited to use as a private residence for a single family/household (which could prevent the Leaseholder 'letting' it on a short term basis via airbnb). If the Flat is situate within a retirement complex then the Lease will contain a restriction to the effect that the Flat can only be occupied by persons over a certain age (usually 55 or 60)

1.3 Alterations

Most Leases contain an absolute restriction on the Leaseholder carrying out structural alterations, as the Landlord or Management Company wish to ensure at all times the structural integrity of the Building. This would not always prevent the Leaseholder from carrying out such alterations (if the Landlord are prepared to allow them) but the Leaseholder would need to obtain the prior consent of the Landlord and, if there is an absolute restriction, they are under no obligation to grant any such consent (and, if they do, they can impose upon the Leaseholder whatever requirements they wish as a part of granting the necessary consent)

In any event, the ability of the Leaseholder to be able to carry out structural alterations will be dependent upon the extent of the Flat demised to them – for instance:

- if the main structural elements are excluded (including the external walls), the Leaseholder is not in a position to carry out alterations to them (such as punching through air vents)
- if the windows are included as part of the demise then their replacement would be a structural alteration requiring the consent of the Landlord or Management Company, but they are much more likely to give such consent provided that the new

windows are similar to those being replaced and in keeping with the remainder of the Building. You should also seek out (and the Landlord or Management Company would usually require) an installer who is registered under either the FENSA Scheme or the CERTASS Scheme, as they will then able to issue their own certificates confirming that the new window installation meets building regulations requirements. If such an installer is not used, then an application will need to be made (by and at the cost of the Leaseholder) to the local planning authority for building regulations approval and their usual process followed

The Lease will usually allow the Leaseholder to carry out internal non-structural alterations to the Flat *with the prior consent of the Landlord or the Management Company* – if the wording I have shown in italics is included within the Lease clause then statute implies that the Landlord or the Management Company are not to unreasonably withhold such consent.

1.4 Disposals (i.e. selling or sub-letting the Flat)

When the Leaseholder purchased the Flat they will have paid a purchase price to the seller, being the value of the Leasehold Flat at the time of the sale – that value will be based upon the then current open market values and also have taken account the length of the Lease Term. The only way the Leaseholder could realise that value is by selling their Leasehold interest in the Flat.

However, some Leaseholders buy Flats as a form of investment (in the hope that property values continue to rise), but do not actually intend to live in them.

In either case it is important to consider what restrictions are contained in the Lease in relation to disposals. By disposals I mean either transferring the Flat to another buyer or to sublet it (i.e. let someone else occupy it).

Many Leases provide for the following:

- no disposals of part only of the Flat – this would prevent subletting individual rooms and/or turning the Flat into a house of multiple occupation
- the transfer of the whole of the Flat to another buyer is permitted
- the granting of subleases of the whole of the Flat, usually by way of an Assured Shorthold Tenancy, is permitted

In some cases, there will be certain requirements of the Landlord or the Management Company which have to be complied with before a Leaseholder can transfer or sublet the Flat such as:

- the prior consent of the Landlord or the Management Company being obtained – if the buyer is a limited company or are based outside the UK then it may be a further requirement that the buyer provides the Landlord or the Management Company with additional security (such as a security deposit or guarantors based in the UK) – so as to ensure that the buyer complies with the Leaseholder's covenants contained in the Lease, as enforceability may be more difficult
- the buyer entering into a Deed of Covenant with the Landlord and the Management Company whereby they agree to comply with the Leaseholder's covenants contained in the Lease
- where appropriate, the buyer to acquire any share the Leaseholder may have in the Management Company or (if there are no such shares) become a member of the Management Company in place of the Leaseholder
- the buyer to serve notice upon the Landlord and the Management Company confirming when the buyer has completed their purchase of the Flat
- the Landlord or the Management Company issuing a certificate confirming that the requirements of the Lease have been met

(which will be needed before the buyer's purchase can be registered at the Land Registry)

A number of these requirements will involve either the Leaseholder or the buyer paying certain fees to the Landlord or the Management Company.

The fees referred to above are generally known as 'Administration Charges' – these sums must be reasonable and the Landlord or the Management Company (as appropriate) must provide a summary of the Leaseholders rights and responsibilities relating to Administration Charges with the demand for payment. If the summary is not included then the charge is not payable until the Landlord or the Management Company issues a demand containing such summary.

Administration Charges would also include:

- fees for or in connection with the provision of information or documents
- fees arising from non-payment of a sum due to the Landlord or the Management Company
- fees arising in connection with a breach (or alleged breach) of the Lease
- (where permitted under the provisions of the Lease), legal costs arising as a result of Court action or a tribunal decision as a result of the Leaseholder (1) failing to pay an amount due to the Landlord or the Management Company or (2) being (or allegedly being) in breach of the term of the Lease

Administration Charges must be reasonable and can be challenged by Leaseholders at the First Tier Tribunal – the Tribunal (or Court) can consider, on application from the Leaseholder, whether it is reasonable for a Landlord to recover all or any part of fees and costs by way of an administration charge.

It should, however, be noted that a Leaseholder cannot make such a challenge against Administration Charges which:

- the Leaseholder has already agreed or admitted responsibility for paying
- have been (or will be) referred to arbitration following a dispute
- have already been decided by a Court or Tribunal

As part of the sale process the Leaseholder usually obtains from the Landlord or the Management Company replies to a Leasehold Property Enquiry Form (known as an LPE1) – this is an industry-wide form which has been drawn up by the various professionals involved with Leasehold property and is designed to give the buyer the comprehensive information they need to assess and understand their purchase (it outlines things such as the service charge payable, provides copy service charge accounts and much more) and is designed to enable the sale process to move much quicker – the cost of this completed form can vary quite a bit and is payable by the Leaseholder.

Potential Reforms

In relation to the sale of Leasehold Flats, the Government has expressed an intention:

- *To set a turnaround time of no more than 15 working days to provide leasehold information to a prospective buyer, and this will be a statutory requirement*
- *To set a maximum fee of £200 plus VAT for producing the replies to the Form LPE1 referred to above – the actual fee charged must reflect the actual cost of providing the LPE1 and is expected to be below the maximum fee, and the Leaseholder will be able to*

challenge unreasonable fees by making an application to the First Tier Tribunal
- A maximum fee of £50 will be payable to the Landlord or Management Company for updating leasehold information – a Lease usually provides that upon completion of a sale the new Leaseholder has to give a formal notice to the Landlord or Management Company confirming completion of the sale and pay a 'registration fee' to them – that fee is usually above £50 and can very often exceed £100!

One point which should be made here is that if the Leasehold Flat is within a retirement complex then the provisions relating to disposals contained in the Lease may well include a requirement for the Leaseholder (as the seller) to pay a specified percentage of the sale price (known as an 'Exit' or 'Event' fee) to the Landlord or the Management Company as well as possibly a further similar contribution towards Service Charge funds. It is very often the case that the Leaseholder is unaware of these fees until the point at which they become payable!

Such provisions are not always limited to sales but can be triggered in unexpected circumstances (such as when a spouse or carer moves into the Flat) and also by sub-lettings (even by way of short term assured shorthold tenancies), where the percentage payable will be based upon the value of the Flat at that time.

Potential Reforms of Exit or Event Fees

The Law Commission, whilst identifying significant problems associated with Exit or Event fees, did not recommend the abolition of such fees but did make numerous recommendations including that such fees are properly regulated

The Government has indicated that it accepts the majority of such recommendations including:

- *The introduction of a new statutory code of practice to regulate such fees*
- *Ensuring that developers and Estate Agents are required to make all such fees crystal clear to buyers before they purchase such properties*

1.5 Payment of Landlord's costs

There is usually an obligation upon the Leaseholder to pay the costs incurred by the Landlord or the Management Company in connection with matters such as:

- service of notices following a breach by the Leaseholder of the obligations contained in the Lease
- applications by the Leaseholder to the Landlord or the Management Company for consent (such as to carry out alterations)
- in the enforcement of the Leaseholder's covenants
- in the recovery of arears due from the Leaseholder

Please see my earlier comments in relation to Administration Charges generally.

1.6 Interest

Most Leases require the Leaseholder to pay to the Landlord or the Management Company interest on late payments of Ground Rent, Service Charge etc. The Lease will specify the rate of interest which will apply and whether it becomes payable as soon as the monies are overdue or whether there is a period of grace (e.g. 14 days late).

1.7 To permit Entry

The Leaseholder usually covenants to allow the Landlord and/or the Management Company (and others) to enter the Flat to inspect, carry out works etc. There is normally a requirement for prior notice to be given (except in case of emergency).

1.8 Dos and Don'ts

All Leases contain a number of 'do and don't' clauses, either included within the main Leaseholder covenants clause but sometimes within a separate clause.

Once again the majority of these will be self-explanatory and will deal with things like:

- keeping pets at the Flat
- erection of satellite dishes
- not to hang washing outside
- not to create noise/nuisance
- parking restrictions

RECOMMENDED ACTION

- Check what obligations you are actually under as set out in your Lease.
- Also make sure what restrictions are imposed upon you in relation to disposing of the Flat. Clearly, if you have bought a Flat on a 'buy to let' basis, you need to make sure that the Lease does not contain any provisions preventing this or provisions which would be very onerous and costly to comply with (bearing in mind that, potentially, you could be subletting the Flat each year to different sub tenants).

Chapter 11

Breach of Covenant by a Leaseholder

If the Leaseholder fails to pay the Ground Rent, Service Charge or any Administration Charges payable under their Lease then the Landlord has various actions open to it including:

- applying to the County Court for a judgement against the Leaseholder
- contacting the Leaseholder's mortgagee and requesting that they pay the monies outstanding, with such mortgagee then adding the amount to the Leaseholder's mortgage debt
- take action to end the Lease (this is known as 'Forfeiture') and repossess the Flat – the Landlord cannot, however, take possession of the Leaseholder's home without a Court Order

As regards to Forfeiture:

- Almost all Leases contain what is known as a 'forfeiture clause' – this is by far the strongest remedy the Landlord has in relation to either non-payment of the Ground Rent (or other sums due under the Lease) or the breach by the Leaseholder of its obligations contained in the Lease – essentially, if successful it allows the Landlord to take back the Flat from the Leaseholder – the Landlord cannot, however, exercise forfeiture if there is no such clause in the Lease.
- Action for forfeiture is commenced by the Landlord by serving upon the Leaseholder a valid notice seeking possession (what is generally known as a 'Section 146 Notice'). In most cases the mere service of such a notice encourages the Leaseholder to pay the sums owed or to make good the breach.
- In view of the severe consequences of this, the ability of the Landlord to exercise such right to forfeit the Lease has been restricted by statute, as briefly shown below:

1. Landlords must now prove that a Leaseholder has broken the terms of the Lease before they can serve a valid Section 146 Notice and such a procedure cannot be used in any event for the recovery of very small sums due
2. Landlords cannot serve a valid Section 146 Notice unless the Leaseholder has agreed that they owe money to the Landlord or that they have breached the terms of the Lease
3. If the Leaseholder has not agreed as above then the Landlord must obtain a determination from the First Tier Tribunal, the Court or an arbitrator that the monies are owed or the Leaseholder has breached the terms of the Lease

Lenders are very uncomfortable with forfeiture clauses, as they stand to lose their security and, if they become aware of the prospect of forfeiture proceedings being started, they often consider paying the outstanding sums themselves or making good the breach, so as to avoid the loss of the property (as mentioned above, they would then add the cost to the Leaseholder's mortgage debt).

Potential Reforms

The Government have requested that the Law Commission report upon possible reforms to the Landlord's right to forfeit a Lease

Chapter 12

Landlord's Covenants

You will not be surprised to see that there are much fewer covenants imposed upon the Landlord than on the Leaseholder! They generally include:

- a covenant for 'quiet enjoyment' – i.e. if the Leaseholder pays the Ground Rent, Service Charge etc. and complies with their obligations contained in the Lease then they should have undisturbed peace and occupation of the Flat
- to insure the Building and the Estate Common Parts (assuming that the Landlord has retained this obligation)
- if there is no Management Company, to maintain the Building and the Common Parts of the Estate and to provide the services (all subject to the Service Charge being paid) and to operate the Service Charge
- if there is a Management Company, to ensure that the Management Company complies with its obligation contained in the Lease and to 'step in' in the event of them not doing so

- to include similar obligations on the part of the relevant Leaseholder in the Leases to be granted of other Flats within the building (i.e. to ensure consistency)
- to enforce covenants against other Leaseholders (at the request and cost of the Leaseholder)

Chapter 13

Management Company Covenants

The covenants imposed upon the Management Company (if there is one) will generally be in relation to the maintenance of the Building and the Common Parts, buildings insurance where applicable, the provision of the services (all subject to the Service Charge being paid) and generally in relation to the operation of the Service Charge.

Management Companies are usually one of the following:

- Independent Management Companies completely separate from the Leaseholders and over which the Leaseholders have no control
- Management Companies in respect of which the Leaseholders are the shareholders in such company, with the Directors and Company Secretary being appointed by such shareholders (i.e. the Leaseholders control such Company)

- Management companies in respect of which the Leaseholders are members (as opposed to shareholders) of such company (i.e. the company does not have a share capital so, instead, the Leaseholders apply to become members) with the Directors and Company Secretary being appointed by such members (i.e. the Leaseholders control such Company)

If the Leaseholders control the Management Company then they also have control over who is appointed to act as Managing Agents on behalf of the Management Company in relation to the performance of the Management Company's obligations and the Service Charge itself.

On some developments (but not all), once the development has been completed either:

- the Freehold Interest in the Building/Estate is transferred to the Management Company by the Landlord or
- the Landlord grants to the Management Company a "Head" Lease of the whole of the Building/Estate

which then creates the situation whereby the Management Company (as well as being responsible for the management of the Building/Estate and its maintenance and the provision of services to it) effectively then becomes the Landlord to the Leaseholders as well, with the Ground Rent then also being payable to the Management Company

Chapter 14

Notices

Many Leases contain a provision which sets out the manner as to how notices are to be served upon the Leaseholder (e.g. recorded delivery, first class post, fax, email) and the Landlord needs to follow these in order for the notice to be effective. These requirements will relate not only to, for example, notices to enter to carry out repair, but also any other notices to be served under the Lease, including in relation to the Service Charge and rent review.

Some Leases do not allow the service of notices etc. by email (are your Service Charge demands sent to you by email – does the Lease allow that?).

Has the Landlord or the Management Company complied with any requirements set out in the Lease as regards to the service of notices?

Chapter 15

Dispute Resolution

Some Leases contain provisions setting out a procedure to be used in the event of disputes between the Leaseholder and the Landlord or Management Company and also between respective Leaseholders within the Building or the Estate.

The First Tier Tribunal (formerly the Leasehold Valuation Tribunal) system was intended to provide Leaseholders with a relatively simple mechanism to deal with certain disputes arising under their Leases with their Landlord or Management Company on a more informal basis than taking them to Court. However, that has not proved to be the case and many Leaseholders have been reluctant to use the system even though they may well have genuine claims – the writer has personal experience of presenting Leaseholders' claims to such a Tribunal and being faced with not only the Landlord's solicitor but also their barrister as well, but even so achieved a successful outcome for the Leaseholders!

Some Landlords are inclined to the view that if they attend the hearing with 'all guns blazing' then:

- the Leaseholders will back down and either not present their claim effectively or will withdraw it altogether or
- the Landlord will be able to convince the Tribunal that there is no merit in the Leaseholder's claim

At present, the Tribunal process is not for the fainthearted (and that should not be the case) but if the claim is presented in the proper way and by determined Leaseholders (on a collective basis) then a satisfactory outcome can be achieved. Nevertheless, the Tribunal system should be made simpler and less confrontational and expensive.

Such Tribunals have, since April 2017, been given the power to determine, on application by the Leaseholder, whether it is reasonable for the Landlord to recover all or any part of their costs by way of Administration Charges.

Potential Reforms

The Government:

- *is considering setting up a new Housing Complaints Resolution Service and is creating a working group to look into and advise in relation to this*
- *has stated its intention to require Freeholders of Leasehold properties to become members of a redress scheme*
- *intends to close legal loopholes relating to the fees payable when Leaseholders take Freeholders to Court*

Chapter 16

Matters Beyond the Lease

Recognised Tenants Association

A Recognised Tenants Association is one where a group of Leaseholders all holding similar leases from the same Landlord within the same Building have joined together to form a Tenants Association to represent their common interests, and such Association has been formally recognised by the Landlord – the Landlord has to give written notice of recognition and, once given, must give 6 months' notice to withdraw such recognition – if the Landlord refuses to give such recognition then the Association can apply to the First Tier Tribunal for a certificate of recognition to be issued.

The Secretary of a Recognised Tenants Association is, with the members consent, able to act on behalf of the members in relation to various issues (some of which are not available to an individual Leaseholder), as follows:

- to ask for a summary of Service Charge costs incurred by the Landlord and in respect of which the members pay a Service Charge

- to inspect relevant accounts and receipts
- to be sent copies of estimates obtained by the Landlord for either long-term agreements to be entered into or intended qualifying works on their properties
- to propose names of contractors to be included in any tender list when the Landlord intends to enter into long-term agreements or carry out qualifying works
- to ask for a written summary of the insurance cover and inspect the policy
- to be consulted about the appointment or re-appointment of a managing agent

In the event of the Landlord disposing of his interest in the Building then a notice needs to be served by the Recognised Tenants Association upon the new Landlord informing them of the existence of the Recognised Tenant's Association and their wish to be consulted about issues in the same manner as before

Statutory Provisions which benefit the Leaseholder

There are a number of Acts of Parliament designed to protect Leaseholders. These can be, understandably, quite complex, and I will not go into them in detail here, so we will only take a very brief look as an outline of what is available.

Landlord and Tenant Act 1985

Section 19 of this Act limits the amount of Service Charge expenditure recoverable:

- to the extent that it is reasonably incurred
- where it is incurred in the provision of services or the carrying out of works, only to the extent that the services or works have been carried out to a 'reasonable standard'

Landlord and Tenant Act 1987 (as amended by the Housing Act 1996)
Part 1 of this Act imposes a duty upon Freeholders of blocks of flats to give the long Leaseholders a 'right of first refusal' when the Freeholder is seeking to dispose of their freehold interest (i.e. giving the Leaseholders the ability to purchase the freehold interest in the block).

Before any such disposal the Freeholder must first serve a formal notice upon such Leaseholders which offers to sell the Freehold in the block of Flats to such Leaseholders and which includes details of:

- the property being offered for sale and the Freeholder's interest in such property
- the principal terms of the sale contract including the amount of the deposit to be payable and the amount of the purchase price to be paid by such Leaseholders
- the period within which the Leaseholders can accept such offer (this must be not less than two months)
- the further period (being not less than two months) within which the Leaseholders may nominate another party to purchase the Freehold interest (usually the Leaseholders would form a Company to act as the purchase 'vehicle')

Until the period set out in such notice for acceptance by the Leaseholders of the offer to sell has expired, the Freeholder is not able to dispose of the property to any other party.

If the Leaseholders do not accept the offer to buy the property, then the Freeholder has a twelve month window in which they can dispose of the property to any other party but only on the basis that the deposit and purchase price payable are not less than those specified in the notice served upon the Leaseholders and that the other terms of the sale correspond with those set out in such notice.

There are slightly different requirements in the event of the Freeholder seeking to dispose of the property at auction.

This Act (Section 24) also gives the Leaseholder, if they are unhappy with the way the Building is being managed, the right to apply to the First Tier Tribunal for an alternative manager to be appointed by them.

The Leasehold Reform, Housing and Urban Development Act 1993

Part I of this Act gave qualifying Leaseholders in blocks of flats:

- the collective right to buy the freehold of their blocks if the Flats are contained in premises that satisfy certain conditions and
- the individual right (where they have held their Lease for 2 years or more) to a new Lease expiring 90 years after the termination of the existing Lease. I have mentioned this in Chapter 6 above

More information in relation to these rights can be found on my web site: www.leaseconsult.co.uk

The Commonhold and Leasehold Reform Act 2002

The provisions of this Act:

- introduced a new form of ownership for blocks of Flats called 'Commonhold', which would allow for the Freehold ownership of Flats. Whilst this form of ownership has not really taken off as yet (as there was considerable reluctance in the market place for it), in January 2021 the Government announced that it was establishing a Commonhold Council with a view to preparing homeowners and the property market for the widespread take up of Commonhold – so it seems that there is now going to be a big push in this direction (although it will only apply to new specially set up developments) – essentially, you will own the freehold interest in your own individual Flat and the rest of the Building/Estate will be jointly managed by the Flat owners

- improved the rights of long Leaseholders in respect of Service and Administration Charges
- introduced restrictions limiting the circumstances in which forfeiture action could be taken for failure to pay Ground Rent
- introduced the concept of Right to Manage Companies (which I refer to in more detail below).

Right to Manage Companies ("RTM")

As mentioned above, the Commonhold and Leasehold Reform Act 2002 gave Leaseholders in blocks of Flats who hold a long Lease of their Flat the ability to group together and collectively take over the management of their block – it is not necessary to demonstrate any fault or failure on the part of the Landlord or their managing agent in order to pursue this and no compensation is payable to the Landlord when the Right to Manage is exercised. There is a set minimum number of 'Qualifying' Leaseholders who must participate in the RTM before it can be exercised, defined procedures and technicalities which have to be followed and certain types of mixed developments are excluded.

Prior to setting out under the RTM procedure, the RTM Company would have to be incorporated (the name of such company must end in 'RTM Company Limited' and the memorandum and articles of association of such company must be in a prescribed form). The Qualifying Leaseholders would be invited to become members of the RTM Company.

In the exercise of the RTM process, in addition to its own costs, the RTM Company is also responsible for the reasonable costs of the Landlord, the manager and any other parties to the Lease in relation to actions taken by them in relation to such RTM claim – in the event of a dispute as to the amount of costs claimed, the issue can be referred to the First Tier Tribunal for a determination.

Once the RTM Company takes over the management, they have the responsibility of choosing and appointing the Managing Agents to assist them in the role and will inevitably appoint a new Managing Agent (sometimes the new Managing Agent helps to guide them through the process).

Since the right to RTM was introduced, a number of difficulties have, however, been experienced by Leaseholders seeking to exercise RTM, where there have been reluctant Landlords and excessive costs, and the current perceived wisdom is that the legislation needs changing to make the process easier and less costly for Leaseholders.

More information in relation to the Right to Manage can be found on my web site: www.leaseconsult.co.uk

Potential Reforms

The Government have expressed the need for the RTM process to be simplified. It has also been suggested that the qualifying criteria for RTM's be relaxed and changes made in relation to the costs payable

The Pledge – there is a commitment to support Leaseholders who wish to take over the collective management of their homes and any communal areas in accordance with leaseholder rights enshrined in legislation

RECOMMENDED ACTION

- If you or your fellow Leaseholders are unhappy at the way your Building is being managed then consider whether any of the provisions of the above Acts of Parliament could help you to improve things
- To try to keep this Handbook relatively short I have deliberately not gone into the provisions of these Acts in any great detail, so further, more detailed, advice would need to be obtained in order to pursue the rights available to you

Chapter 17

Managing Agents

Not all Managing Agents are professionally qualified or are members of a recognised trade body.

As regards to professional qualification, the relevant bodies are:

- The Institute of Residential Property Management
- The Royal Institution of Chartered Surveyors ("RICS")
- The Chartered Institute of Housing (in the social housing sector)

Recognised trade bodies are:

- The Association of Residential Managing Agents ("ARMA")
- RICS
- The Association of Retirement Housing Managers ("ARHM")

By being a member of a professional body or a recognised trade body, the Managing Agents will be required to comply with the regulations laid down by such organisations, including:

- Regular audits to ensure that such regulations are being followed
- A requirement for them to hold suitable professional indemnity insurance and fidelity insurance
- Specific requirements as to how they must hold Clients' monies
- A suitable complaints procedure and membership of and access to an independent dispute resolution scheme

There are two Codes of Practice which apply to the management of residential Leasehold property and which have been approved by the Government:

- the Service Charge residential management Code (3rd Edition) produced by the Royal Institution of Chartered Surveyors
- the Private Retirement Housing Code of Practice for England produced by the Association of Retirement Housing Managers

Whilst I acknowledge that the amount payable to them (which is usually assessed by the Managing Agent on the basis of a specified sum per Flat) will be a factor in appointing a Managing Agent, this should not be the only driving factor – sometimes Managing Agents achieve a lower fee by spreading themselves too thin and take on too many properties to manage and thereby fail to interpret the requirements of the Lease or manage any of them properly or effectively – for example, they may not build up a reserve fund by way of annual contributions from all Leaseholders with the disastrous consequence that in the event of major works being necessary, say the replacement of the roof of the Building or replacement of the lift, the Leaseholders will have to contribute towards such costs (which would be substantial) all in one go!

Potential Reforms

- The Government have committed to regulating Managing Agents with a single mandatory and legally enforceable Code of Practice
- Managing Agents will be required to have a nationally recognised qualification to practice
- The Government wishes to empower Leaseholders to switch Managing Agents where they perform poorly or break the terms of their contract, as well as simplify the Right to Manage process

RECOMMENDED ACTION

- If the Leaseholders control the Management Company then it is open to them to seek to change the Managing Agents (as the Managing Agents act on behalf of the Management Company) – only the Directors and Secretary of the Management Company would be able to do this on instruction from the shareholders or members of the Management Company
- Check the terms of the Management Agreement (i.e. the contract between the Management Company and the Managing Agents in relation to the management of the Building) to see how long it runs for and what needs to be done in order to terminate such contract
- Do some research and seek to find alternative Managing Agents who are not solely focused on making a profit but also has the Leaseholder's interests (and the issues mentioned in this Handbook) in mind – also ask them how long it takes to produce year end accounts

Chapter 18

Cladding on Buildings – Post Grenfell

This is a matter which continues to cause great concern to a number of Leaseholders, as the ramifications of the tragic events at Grenfell Tower become clearer and steps taken to ensure the safety of the Leaseholders and occupiers in buildings containing Leasehold Flats.

In keeping with the nature of this Handbook, I will only deal with this subject relatively briefly, but that does not mean that I do not recognise the seriousness of the issue and I have included below details of where further help and assistance are available.

In many cases, it has become necessary for works to be carried out including the replacement of non-compliant cladding. Such works are known as "remediation works". Associated inspections have also revealed the need for additional safety works to be carried out (the cost of which is quite substantial) and that has given rise to the question "who is to pay for the cost of all these works?"

The starting point should be that when the relevant building was constructed it would have needed to comply with the planning and building regulations (including fire safety) as they applied at the time of construction and the building would have ultimately been 'signed off' by the local authority and, where appropriate, had NHBC cover.

However, account also has to be taken of the terms of the Lease held by the respective Leaseholder (particularly the Service Charge obligations imposed upon the Leaseholder) and there has been at least one case where the First Tier Tribunal has ruled (on the facts of that particular case) that the cost of the remediation works was recoverable from the Leaseholders – there was, however, a successful outcome for those Leaseholders as the original developer ultimately agreed to cover the cost of the remediation works and associated costs.

Some other developers have since also agreed to cover such remediation costs in relation to buildings which they built, but there are still many cases where the Freeholders or Landlords of affected buildings believe that the remediation costs should fall upon the Leaseholders.

In another instance NHBC has accepted a claim for the cost of remediation works.

The issue of who is to pay for such remediation costs remains a matter of contention.

Initially, the then Government took the view that it would be unacceptable for Leaseholders in affected private blocks to pay the cost of such remediation works (although many Landlords, Freeholders and Developers, unsurprisingly, took a different view!). In 2019 the Government confirmed that they would fully fund the replacement of unsafe aluminium composite material ("AMC") cladding on high rise private residential properties where building owners have failed to do so. A deadline of 31 December 2019 was placed on submitting applications for such funding and it was expected that the AMC cladding would have been replaced by June 2020. That expectation was before Covid 19 and this has clearly had an impact – as at 31 October 2020 it appeared that only 64% of privately owned buildings had started or completed such remediation process.

It has also become apparent that there are many other buildings which have unsafe cladding which is not AMC and in March 2020 the Government committed to providing £1 billion of funding in 2020 to 2021 to support the remediation of unsafe non-ACM cladding systems on residential buildings 18 metres and over in height, in both the private and social housing sectors.

The registration process for this Building Safety Fund opened on 1 June 2020 and closed on 31 July 2020. Applications for funding are only being considered by the Government from building owners, freeholders or responsible entities who registered, with the deadline for submitting funding applications being December 2020. The deadline for applications to this fund has subsequently been extended to 30 June 2021.

The general view is that the funding currently proposed by the Government will not be anywhere near enough to cover the cost all of the remediation works needed.

The position is further complicated by the fact that, subsequently, the Government has changed its view, in relation to who should fund the cost of remediation works, from that as outlined above to the suggestion that Leaseholders should be protected from "unaffordable costs" (i.e. they will now be expected to make a contribution). That is a dramatic change and has led to calls for Leaseholders to be properly protected, as they have been put in a position not of their making, and pressure groups being formed to fight this battle on behalf of Leaseholders.

The Government has subsequently bowed to increasing pressure with an announcement in December 2020 that it is expecting the building industry to contribute towards remediation costs.

More and more pressure is being brought to bear upon the Government to resolve the issue in a manner which does not involve passing the huge costs involved on to Leaseholders.

One of the leaders in this fight are the Leasehold Knowledge Partnership (www.leaseholdknowledge.com) and I strongly recommend that any Leaseholder who is suffering from this issue visits their web site.

Potential Reforms

Fire Safety Bill – as part of its response to dealing with the issues raised by Grenfell, the Government has introduced this Bill with a view to enhancing fire safety in buildings containing more than one home. The main thrust of the Bill is to clarify the extent of the buildings and parts of such buildings which are subject to the Regulatory Reform (Fire Safety) Order 2005 (which consolidates the main fire safety regulations) by making it clear that for any building containing two or more sets of domestic premises that Order will apply to the building's structure and external walls and any common parts and all doors between the domestic premises and common parts. It has been stated that these clarifications are important to:

- Ensure that owners or managers of multi-occupied residential buildings include an assessment of risk related to fire and fire spread in respect of these parts of the relevant premises. As a result, such persons will be under a duty to take general fire precautions to ensure the premises are safe to those lawfully there
- Affirm that Fire and Rescue authorities can take enforcement action against such owners and managers if they have failed to comply with their duties under the Fire Safety Order in relation to these parts of such premises

At the time of writing this Handbook, the House of Commons were yet to consider proposed amendments made to the draft Bill by the House of Lords

Building Safety Bill – the Government is also introducing this draft Bill with the expressed aim (amongst other things) to:

- *establish a new Building Safety Regulator, who will oversee the safety and performance of all buildings and actively oversee and enforce a more stringent regulatory regime for buildings in scope during their design, construction and occupation*
- *introduce a more stringent regime to all multi-occupied residential buildings of 18 metres or more in height, or more than six storeys (whichever is reached first), with potential for that to be extended further*
- *give the Regulator responsibility for major regulatory decisions, including whether to allow a building to be constructed and later occupied*
- *establish a system of duty holders, who will be responsible for showing compliance with the regulations at three stages – (1) before planning permission is granted (2) before construction begins and (3) before occupation*
- *during occupation, establish two roles – the Accountable Person and the Building Safety Manager*
- *introducing the requirement that, before occupation, a building must have a Building Registration Certificate which must detail the Accountable Person and the Building Safety Manager*
- *a mandatory requirement for the submission of a safety case to the Regulator (based upon risk assessments), which the Building Safety Manager will be required to keep up to date*
- *establish a regime of enforcement measures in order to ensure compliance*

RECOMMENDED ACTION

If you are affected by the cladding issue, it is very important that you seek suitable professional advice – before incurring costs for such advice, the best place to start should be the free advice and information available via the following web sites:

- the Leasehold Advisory Service web site (www.lease-advice.org)
- the Leasehold Knowledge Partnership web site (www.leaseholdknowledge.com)

LKP are also actively engaged in pursuing changes in Leasehold Law generally, for the better protection of all Leaseholders

Cladding replacement and remediation costs is very much an area where a collective approach by all Leaseholders who are having to deal with this issue will be much more effective.

Chapter 19

Making Landlord and Tenant Law Easier

The current law has evolved over many years and is the subject of various Acts of Parliament. Most of those working within this field believe that it would be beneficial for the law to be improved and simplified for the benefit and protection of Leaseholders.

A suggestion has been made that there should be one model form of Lease for all, which could then be supplemented with additional provisions to be attached in order to make the Lease specific to a particular Building/Estate – whilst this is a noble idea, from past experience the writer believes that it is probably doomed to failure as many Landlords will just seek to add to the 'standard Lease' so many pages of additional provisions that the simplicity and uniformity of the Lease will be lost!

Potential Reforms

The Government are proposing to deal with the potential reforms mentioned earlier in this Handbook in two stages

As mentioned above, some of the necessary legislation is intended to be introduced quickly (such as in relation to the setting of future Ground Rents to zero), whereas the others will take longer

The Government's stated objective is to achieve the biggest reforms to English property law for 40 years